Gillian Tye.

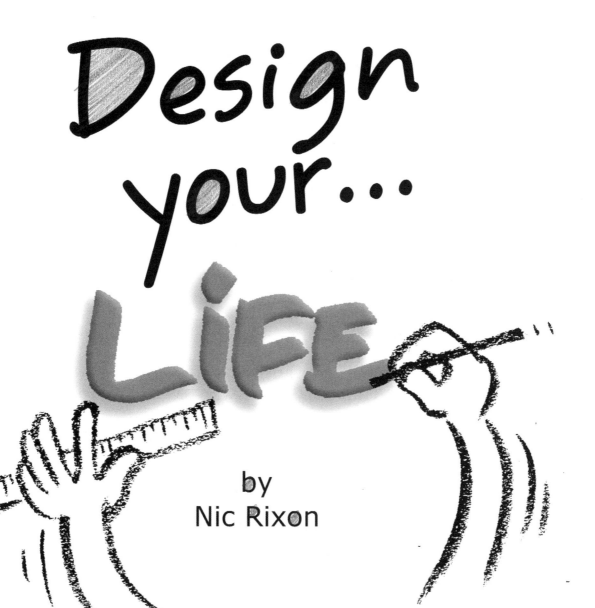

Design your... LIFE

by
Nic Rixon

Design your Life
by Nic Rixon

www.nic-rixon.com

First published in Great Britain in 2003 by
Filament Publishing
14, Croydon Road, Waddon,
Croydon, Surrey CR0 4PA
0208 688 2598
www.filamentpublishing.com

Text copyright Nic Rixon © 2003
Ilustrations by Terry Christian © 2003

Printed by Antony Rowe, Chippenham & Eastbourne
Design & Layout by David Fowler, DNF Creative

A CIP catalogue record for this book is available
from the British Library

ISBN 0-9546531-0-6

Index of Contents

Index continued

Foreword

Early in 1999, I was told about a trainer called Nic Rixon. "You'll be impressed!",
I was told. In October I met him for the first time and he presented on The Coaching
Academy's first ever training programme. It was then that I discovered that impressed
was an understatement - I was gobsmacked by the impact he made on an audience
who had already seen the highest rated speakers in the world.

They went away talking about Nic in a way that I had not seen before: not only were
they impressed with the contents of his session, but were blown away by his energy
and enthusiasm.

The contents of this book are the results of teaching thousands of our coaches this
essential coaching tool. I do not believe that you will find anywhere a more exhaustive,
in depth treatment of the subject, or indeed have the opportunity to learn from such
a master trainer.

One final thought: see Nic Rixon live, as soon as you can.
Then you can be gobsmacked too!

I am proud that he is a tutor with The Coaching Academy

Jonathan Jay
Managing Director
The Coaching Academy UK Ltd

The Best Goal Setting Tool Ever !

All of the skills to change your world are in you, not this book. What _is_ in this book, is a framework to help you discover, align, and focus all those skills.

"The smartest person we know, is the person who asks our advice" Which makes you...?

My thanks to Jonathan Jay. Managing Director and Founder of the Coaching Academy, who has given me much encouragement, support, and inspiration, as part of the Coaching Academy's training team. Jonathan is one of those unique people, who have built an incredibly successful business, starting with not much more than an idea, and virtually created a new industry at the same time. One of the Uks true entrepreneurs. Without the opportunity to work with you, this book would probably, never have been written.

There are additional people I would like to thank, for all sorts of reasons, and I have done so at the end of this book. The reason, the end ? Well, long thank yous, should be placed where the people most interested in them, can find them, at the end of the book. That thought is based on the belief, that at least all of the people I've thanked, will read the book. I hope one or two other people will as well, and if you are one of them,

...Thank you.

I started writing this book in response to all the people who were kind enough to tell me they had enjoyed my seminar, or had heard me speak at The Coaching Academy weekend, or various seminars, or had listened to my tapes and, as a result of the experience, had made some changes in their lives and wanted to know more. Some just needed to know one more thing, or had one small technical question they needed clarity on, (I speak at 300 + words a minute so we cover a lot of ground) and could I just tell them where they could get my book, or ' is there a hand out ?'.

So, for those of you who were confident enough in me, and my ability to express myself with the written word, to believe I had written a book....

Here it is !

What's it all about

I have no great plan for this book, other than it should give you the tools it has taken me twenty years to shape,

In -
The shortest possible time
And -
The simplest, and easiest possible way to understand and use. And I'm only interested in you designing your life exactly the way you want it, and you being happy.

So I hope that's ok!
(maybe that is a great plan after all.)

Now I'm a speaker, not a writer, so I'll write this like I'd say it, so don't bother trying to pick holes in my grammar, I never learned the rules proper any how!

And this program is giving me enough advice as it is.

I also hope you will allow me to turn over a few of my personal stones along the way, in the search for the inspiration that kept me going through the tough times, and drove me when I needed it. To that end I will scatter through this book, the stories (some my own), "quotes," one liners, and in some cases, jokes that have amused, challenged and motivated me along the way. First I have to tell you, I have overcome no great disaster. I have suffered no huge loss. I didn't lose my business and go spectacularly broke. My wife and kids didn't leave me and I haven't pulled myself out of the pit of despair so I could tell you my story in all its gory details.

— INSPIRATION —

So if you're looking for, "Hell and Back Again" ...wrong book

I don't want to take anything away from those people who've done any of those things though and if your personal circumstances find you in one of those places today, then I hope this book will give you some ideas and tools so that you can rise above your own personal challenges. And one day you will tell me your story of triumph over adversity.

Here's my thought though, as I sat in an audience

many years ago, listening to a man who had returned from "TERRIBLE" circumstances. He had lost everything, his business had gone bust, his wife and kids had left him, and he had also lost his house and all his possessions. My heart went out to him, 'cos I gotta tell ya in twenty years in business, as a family man, I've stared into the abyss once or twice myself along the way.

Yet as I sat there I couldn't help thinking that the person I really wanted to hear from, was the one who had faced all of those problems and dealt with them successfully. The person who had just celebrated their 50th wedding anniversary with their partner and all the kids and grand kids, the one who had retired exactly when they wanted to, having enjoyed every step along the way, to continue to do what they loved, in good health with a fat bank balance, just because they could, rather than because they had to. Now that was what I wanted to do, if I could live my life that way, live happy, be happy, I would have everything . When you think of the percentage of failed relationships and businesses today, there's already too many people good at getting it wrong. Now I freely admit I was probably thinking of a man retiring there, but I'd also like to meet the woman who helped him do it. Actually this might be the time to tell you one of my favourite Zig Ziglar stories. I'm not sure if it's entirely true in this case. I know in my own life it is, and I'm sure in many of yours to. (By the way if I screw up the whole sexist political correctness thing, for HIS read HERS, for HERS read HIS . For SHE insert LINDA, for chicks and babes,

get over it...   ...oh yeah... forgive me)

So... the story, the Mayor of New York was visiting a building site with his wife, and whilst they were there it became obvious that she, (not Linda this time) had had a romantic relationship with the head of the construction site when they had been at school together. As the Mayor and his wife left, he turned to her and said " There you go honey, if you'd married him you'd be the wife of a construction worker. And she said " No, if I'd married him, he'd be Mayor"

Now if you're a man reading this, just read that story again, then if you want some brownie points read it to your girlfriend or if you're married, your wife, or better still your mum, hey even your sister. If you are a woman reading this at least you know one of us knows!!

You're glad you didn't throw the book away after "Chicks & Babes" now, aren't you.

Where are you now ?

The stage of your life this book finds you in...
will affect how you view the information in it.
Like the seasons our lives go through stages and
changes. You may be in the spring time of your life, or
opportunity, just starting out on your own, and you're full
of excitement and unstoppability. You may be a mum
whose kids are off to school, or off on their own life
journey and you're dipping your toe back in the job
market, or dreaming of starting your own business. You
might have taken early retirement and are looking for
something new to do, or you might be like I was,
"ordinary bloke seeks new meaning". You may even be at
the bottom of your own personal
spiral and are looking
for the tools to reverse
your fortune.

So you've made your move, or reached
a decision and along with a little
trepidation you're excited at
all the new possibilities.

I hope this book, and the tools in it, will help you
avoid some of the pitfalls I have plummeted into
with gay abandon.

You may be in the autumn of your particular situation and are enjoying the fruits of all your labours, but looking for some new challenge, or you may be looking ahead to winter, and it's looking a bit bleak and you need a little motivation.

Whatever your situation, together, we'll shorten the way, and lighten the load and wherever this book finds you, good times or tough times, you've picked it up for a reason. So, _now_ is the right time.

"May the best of your past,
be the worst of your future."

Let's get acquainted

For those of you who don't have a clue who I am (and why should you), I'm the ordinary bloke who lives next door. I have a wonderful wife and partner in life, Linda. Two amazing kids Emily and Oliver (not a Kevin in sight, ever!) At the time of writing this, they are 19 and 18 respectively. Which reminds me, we used to have a sign up in our reception at work, which said;

"Employ a teenager... whilst they still know everything"

I have a great relationship with my mum and dad. Although I never did work out how my dad was so dumb when I was 13 and got to be so smart when I turned 20. So, I am living in anticipation of my own massive I.Q. expansion during the next couple of years, when my kids discover how brilliant their father really is. I suppose it's part of growing up.

I also get on really well with my Mother in Law.
"Hang on a minute, I thought you said ordinary bloke!"

Oh yeah... I go shopping with
Linda too... and have a blast!

I have businesses in manufacturing, property and training. I started the first 20 years ago in 1983 and still have it today and as I am writing this I am about to launch a new "Business Coaching," business.

Having spent the first 5 years in business finding out what I <u>didn't</u> know about everything, I spent the next 15 years studying business skills, people skills, NLP and coaching, plus any other tool or book or advisor I could learn one good idea from, trying to find the answer.

I qualified as a Dale Carnegie instructor 12 years ago, which if you haven't heard of him, may not mean anything to you.

Although most people have heard of his book, "How to Win Friends and Influence People" which is the book that started me on my journey.

I have been involved in training 3000 + life coaches as part of "The Coaching Academy" training team and have trained, been guest speaker to, or coached over 10,000 people.

...So that's me.

Now I don't know exactly what you want, with your life or your future, but I'll take a guess, that like many of the people who come up to me at seminars, or write to me, you don't know what you want either, or you know what you want, and don't know how to get it. Or, you got a whole bunch of stuff you _DON'T_ want in your life and don't know how to get rid of it !

Wadaya reckon... Am I close ?...
....Thought so.

Good news bulletin

Nobody ever changed things from a position of satisfaction. If they're ok with it they leave it alone; things have got to get pretty bad before anybody does anything. People have to get frustrated and pissed off first. They don't get to the "pinch-an-inch" stage and rush down the gym and join Weight Watchers, they get to the "grab-a-handful" stage. And then spend a year at the "I really should" stage until its two handful's and then, in frustration shout Enough!
And go do something.

They don't have two cross words with their spouse, and phone Relate, they do it when there's no crockery left to smash. So, if you are more than a little frustrated right now ...

... Good ...
... You're ready.

Even people who are doing great can still get frustrated looking for a better, faster, easier way. And the more frustrated you are the faster you will put the ideas in this book into practice, and the quicker things change.

I am excited to be with you on this journey. I have picked some of the most powerful tools and distinctions I've collected along the way, the ones that have had the most impact on me. The ones that have enabled me to make the greatest change and improvements, in both my life, and the lives of the people I've coached using these tools. I'm sure, with a little effort, you'll find the same value we did.

Rule Number 1
There aren't really any rules.

You do need, however to be a seeker. Now you've already got that one down pat, or you wouldn't have picked up this book.

Seek and ye shall find. I know... you've heard it before, but here's the most important bit, Finding is reserved for the seekers. Very few people, if any, wander into work, stroll about, do a bit here and a bit there, and wind up chairman of the board. People who got it, usually, not always, but usually, wanted it, whatever "<u>IT</u>" may be, and as we travel this road of self discovery together, you will start to realise that goes for the bad stuff too.

WHERE?... WHERE?...

Example...

Now this doesn't apply to <u>YOU</u> and <u>ME</u>, we're smarter than that, but we know people who always have too much month left at the end of their money. They always know who did what to whom on the latest soap though. Because instead of getting an evening job, or going to night school to get a better job to pay the bills, they chose to sit in front of the telly instead.

We, (not you-n-me) the collective we, watch on average, 25 hours of TV a week. Now I'm not a great lover of average, because you can have one hand in a bowl of boiling water and one frozen in a block of ice, and on average you won't be happy. So let's just say we probably have some time available that could be spent more wisely.

We also know people, who are overweight by choice, now I can't speak for you, but as far as I'm concerned, I've never accidentally eaten anything, it was always by choice. If I choose to eat too much today I have chosen to weigh too much tomorrow.

I think I've accidentally swallowed a goat!

It's my choice ! So the end goal of these tools is to help you and, if you're coaching, your clients, make the right choices.

A couple of my favourite thoughts on this, I was once asked if I like to eat a lot. To which I answered... Yep, and I was told...ok so eat a little, that way you get to live a long time, and eat a lot. The other was from my daughter, which was "Chocolate makes your clothes shrink"

Does that help at all ?
Not even a bit ?... Oh well.

So be a seeker, never give up looking for a way to get where you want to go. Keep your mind open, for the new idea, the new book, the next seminar, the one distinction that will take your life in a whole new direction, and to a whole new level.

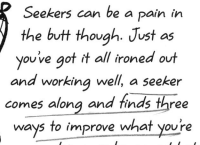

Seekers can be a pain in the butt though. Just as you've got it all ironed out and working well, a seeker comes along and finds three ways to improve what you're doing, so be a world class seeker, find new ways to use the material in this book, adapt it to your situation, it will make a huge difference provided you...

Take Action

When I first started my own Journey, I thought I was looking for the Grail of personal enlightenment, and when I found it, everything would magically change, and my life would be perfect. I know... you live and learn. (Or you never really live)

One of the things that has always fascinated and frustrated me is the people in my seminars and workshops who say, "I know what to do, but I don't do what I know" and I say... **"Why Not !"**

I remember one of my own moments of discovery, I had been driving around with a "Romance After Marriage" relationship tape in the tape player in my car. Linda was sitting next to me and I'm thinking, oooh she always does that, or ah ha ! she never does that, or why won't she say this or do that, whinge moan whine in my own head.

My focus was, I hope she's listening to this because <u>SHE</u> needs to change. I know, I know, as I'm writing this, even I can't believe I was such a plonker. Two or three weeks down the road I was out on my own in the car, and flipped on the tape, no Linda in the car, so I had to listen for myself, and I thought, sssssooo (breath in when you do that one) I don't do that. Ooooh I always do that. Oh no, I know I should do that. Well I suppose it wouldn't hurt to try that, or help out with that. So I changed. I started doing <u>SOME</u> (Just a man, feet of clay n all that) of the things I should, and stopped doing <u>SOME</u> (Ditto) of the things I shouldn't and the most amazing thing happened, when I showed up as a different person, she (Linda) showed up differently too. I didn't do it so she would, I'd made up my mind to do it because it was the right thing to do. When I changed, I looked at the world through a different pair of eyes, and <u>EVERYTHING</u> was different.

I truly believe I would not be married to this amazing woman today, had I not made that choice.

Go on... CHANGE!

19

I'm also quite pleased with myself, as a bloke, as it only took me about 5 years to get into the mess in the first place, and 18 months to figure it out, and sort it.

"The biggest room in the world, is the room for self improvement"

So when you get an idea, or a new concept, try it out, don't wait until you're perfect. Give it a go, look at the result you get, adjust your approach and try again, and if, just when you think you're getting it right, along comes the seeker looking for a better way.

celebrate !

Linda once asked me "aren't you ever satisfied "
(steady now) I'm not even sure where my answer came from, but I said, "Nope... I'd be finished then"

Remember...

A thing worth doing is worth doing badly, until you can learn to do it better.

Take action NOW !!

what's the worst that can happen ???

20

The Main thing is to keep the main thing, the main thing.

There are so many things I have learnt along the way, from both experience and brilliant people, and I would love to share them all with you now, but they will have to wait for other books and other seminars, as the next tool is the main reason for this book.

It was the tool that changed my life...
...and saved my ass.

The frustrations that were plaguing me at that time were the normal ones. I was broke, I owed the bank £150,000 not including my mortgage I had just posted losses for the year of £40,000 and it looked like we may lose the house and have to take the kids out of school. I was at least 2 stone overweight, and had had the "is there any point to this marriage" conversation with Linda.
I was working 14 to 16 hours a day, and I remember one week where we worked 5 days and nights without stopping, just to get enough work out to pay the wage bill for that month.

ZONK!

So I was close to "Hell and back again" and
I hated my Life.

Within a year we had improved the profit in the business to £500,000 The foundations of a life time best friendship were in place with Linda (I am still working on that, and I think I'm getting better)

I lost 2 stone and 6 inches off my waist, in 4 weeks, dropped 2 hours sleep a night, and got rid of my headaches. (Had to take a bottle of pills some months just to be able function)

We sold the house and moved closer to the business, and the process I went through (which you're about to go through) saves me 10 hours a week, not including the time I saved with the reduced journey, and has done so since that day.

And now I love my Life. (and Wife)

So if any of that strikes a chord with you, read on, but be prepared to take...

...Massive action.

Know what you really want

I'm not talking about what you think you want, or what
your spouse said you should want, or what your best mate
said you ought to try doing. I mean what you really
want, for yourself.... And you say

"IF I KNEW THAT I WOULDN'T NEED THIS BLASTED BOOK" ...

" ain't dat de truth "

So here's the problem, there's no button on your computer
you can push, no TV station broadcasting the answer, no
web site, no mate, no magazine
quiz that can point you in the
right direction. The only
person who knows what you
want, is of course, you. The
problem is, it's not your
conscious mind that knows
the answer, but your
subconscious mind.
Which is great because what
I found, and subsequently further developed
(ahh! tis the seeker in me!) is a tool for talking to
the subconscious mind, and you're about to use it.

Firstly this process takes time, so, don't expect to spend two hours doing this and have everything fixed. This is the start of living a new way ...on purpose.

Enough Philosophy Rixon. Get on with it !

Get yourself a piece of paper and draw a circle to the approximate proportions shown in the diagram.

Or use the page provided, by the way, the reason there are such large margins is not because I have shares in a paper mill, it's so you can jot down your thoughts as you go through this book.

Personalise it, capture your ideas, sketch new ways to use the concepts, write your own quotes, add your own drawings, it's a work book, use it.

...IT'S A WORK BOOK!

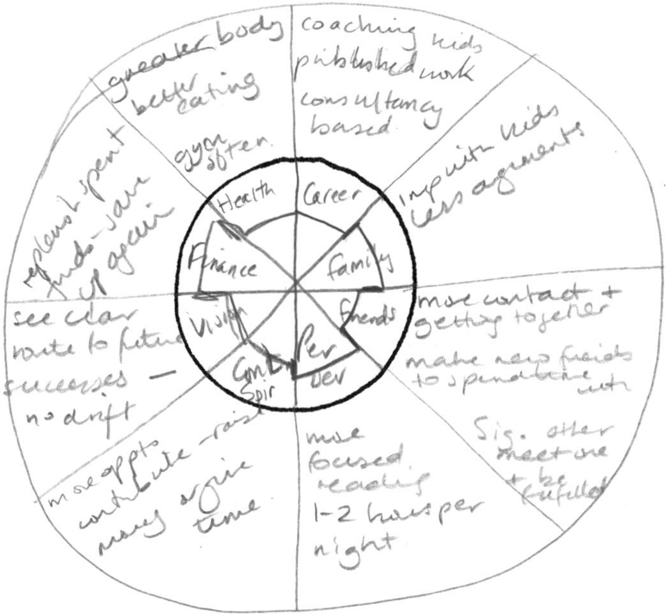
Health
Career
Family
Friends
Per Dev
Spir
Vision
Finance
greater body
better eating
gym often
coaching kids
published work
consultancy based
less arguments
more contact + getting together
Sig. other
meet one
+ be fulfilled
more
focused
reading
1-2 hours per
night
time
see clear
route to future
successes —
no drift

Yours could start like this....

Then divide it into 8 segments, if you have done this exercise before make sure you don't look at your old wheel. Do a new one from scratch... ...Why?

Because things change, and you need to know what's important to you, today. If you are a coach looking to use this for your clients, do it for yourself first, you need to experience the power of it, before you can ask someone else to use it.

Reminds me of a good friend of mine, who was selling me the idea that I must try skiing, "Oh man, the clear blue sky, crisp clear air and this amazing feeling of charging down the mountain on clean soft white powder snow, Nic it's fantastic, you gotta try it". Man, I was sold. So, I asked, where did you go ? "Oh" he said...

...''I've never been skiing'' !**@>*%$$&@

When your clients ask you what difference the wheel made to your life, make sure you can tell em truly what you gained, be congruent in your communication, give them the facts, add the passion if it was there. If it changed your life, your focus, your outcomes, let them know what that meant to you.

(Wait a minute Nic! You mean all that could happen if I do all the work in this book) Yep !

So, in each segment write in one of the areas of your life that is important to you.

I'll get you started... Health or Career ... Might be two.

List all the areas that come into your mind, if you have more than eight, just subdivide one of the segments. If you have a lot more draw two wheels. If you get stuck at four or five, there is a list of some of the potential areas over the page. Don't Look Yet, !

Give yourself, and your subconscious mind, time to find the areas that are important to YOU Otherwise you'll end up working on the areas that are important to me.

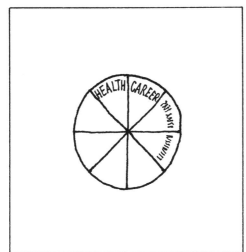

Ok so did you turn over before you really tried, if you did you're busted, try again. If you really are stuck the list is on page...... 96

Ok, If you have a full wheel, its time to evaluate.

The centre of the wheel equates to 0 the rim is 10.
0 = the worst it could be. 10 = the best it could be.

Mark your current level of satisfaction with each area

But....

Now don't hear what I didn't say. 10 should only represent the best you COULD be TODAY, not the best you could ever be.

Example...

If you just got fired for not showing up for work, and you're 35 and highly qualified, and should be office manager by now, you would probably mark your career section 0 If, however you just had your review and they told you, you were doing ok in some areas but need to improve in some others, you might be a 6 or 5 It's a gut feel thing, do it fast, let your subconscious make the decisions.

I know all you perfectionists out there are freaking out now, "

"what ! there's no right way" ! that's right, just trust your intuition.

Actually I have a little perfectionist story for you, it was when Linda and I did the Individual ropes course which involved climbing a 50' telegraph pole on our own. We were told by the instructors that as we climbed onto the top of the pole we would be tempted to grab the safety wire (which was attached to an overhead wire, and our safety harness), to steady ourselves as we stood up, as there was nothing else to grab onto. So, I go up, get to the top which is quite an accomplishment for me as I am not good with heights. (in fact I could not have done this at all had it not been for an experience earlier the same year, more of that later)
Sure enough I grab for the wire, but I'd seen everyone else do it, so what the hell. I stood straight up took a photo with a disposable camera, threw it down to my team and jumped for the trapeze about ten feet away,

(oop's did I forget the trapeze)

caught it and hung on for a moment. I was too exhausted at this stage to do anything clever, so I let go, and the safety rope handlers lowered me to my team.

Two hours later it's Linda's turn, she gets into her safety harness and up she goes. Linda has no fear of heights and gets to the top quite easily, but now comes the hard bit, she gets as high as she can, gets one foot up onto the top, starts to stand up and is lifting the other foot up and she starts to lose her balance. I watch her reach up to grab the safety rope and I can almost hear her saying to herself "no that's not the right way, to do it perfectly I mustn't grab the rope" So in slow motion I watch her snatch her hand away, and fall. The safety guys lower her to the ground, and I fight my way through the crowds at the base of the poles. When I get to her, there's some trainer in her face asking what that meant to her. She was distraught, upset, crying and furious with herself all at the same time. Finally I wrest her away from the trainer and give her a hug.

"I should have grabbed the damn rope" she says to me

What did that teach you I said ?

"That I damn well always have to do it bloody right!"

So I said "what does that stop you doing?"

And she freezes and looks at me, with this stunned expression on her face, and says "oh god... Nic everything... It stops me doing everything..." And she grabs me, so I hold her until she stops crying and after a few moments she starts sobbing and laughing at the same time, because she suddenly realises... she's free of it, she's let it go, and it only took 45 years.... This won't be the last time I say this, anything worth doing, is worth doing badly... until you can learn to do it better.

Now, if you haven't already, draw a line across each segment where you have scored it and it should look something this, and be completely happy that there is no perfect answer, just your best guess.

Whether this is your first time working with the wheel, or you've done this before, you may well be feeling the same way I did when I had completed my wheel for the first time. I was <u>DEPRESSED</u>, this represented a measurement of my misery, no way to avoid it, there it was, written down, and trust me when I did mine it

didn't look anywhere as good as the diagram.
The first time I worked through this exercise with a
group of people, I watched the expression on their
faces as they looked at their finished wheel, and
my brain went into overdrive, and I thought I can't
leave them there.

" They looked suicidal "

What follows...

...the wheel you're about to use, was developed on the
spot, with a room of about 85 people, it just seemed to
flow. Sure I polished it up later, but the magic happened
in that moment. I think it was that or get lynched by
85 depressed life coaches. It was one of those special
moments when you know there's a purpose to what you
do, and why you are here.

The stories that come back to me, from people who have completed this process are quite amazing, and inspirational. I may well include one or two along the way. So whether you're looking at your wheel and feeling good or depressed right now, you didn't pick up this book to stay where you are, so stick with me, my story gets better.

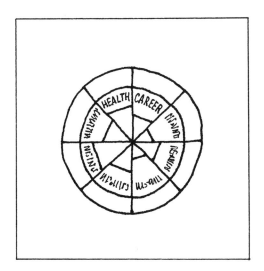

Draw a larger wheel around the first one, (see diagram), extending the spokes as shown, and in each of these new segments, write a brief description of what 10 would look like or feel or be like, or one outcome you would like.

For example if you have a "family" segment one outcome might be to have a conversation with your dad and not argue, or to tell him you love him, or think the world of him. Maybe it could be to listen to your daughter without judging.

(Hey I didn't say
it would be easy)

For the guys reading this I can not tell you how much my life improved when I learned my wife and my daughter did not need fixing, they needed listening to, that's all the way to the end of their sentence, and then you wait for at least 15 seconds, 20 if it's a biggy, because they start again, don't offer advice, if they ask you what to do, ask them what _THEY_ think they should do, then its back to listening.

Give it a try, you might learn something.

One of the main complaints of newly divorced women is:
" he didn't listen to me "

You could help by preframing us. When you just need our ears, tell us you just want us to listen. Let us know you don't want us to fix anything, you don't think it's our fault, you just want someone to talk to. Hey its gotta be worth a shot, and remember we're men, we only do one thing at a time, so if you ask us to think about something don't expect us to start talking about it until we've finished thinking about it.

If you are a woman reading this,
" I'm working on 'em girls"

If you're a Guy
"try it"

34

Another examples of an outcome, in a health segment, might be to be X stone by a certain date. To have stopped smoking by... to be booked into a gym and attending regularly, by...

... You get the idea.

So go to it, a good description of 10 and as many outcomes as you can think of.

20 mins to an hour "tops"
....GO!

Beliefs

Some times we need to work on our belief system. We need to open our minds to the possibility, that we can learn, and do much more than we ever thought possible, because......

"People will not rise above their own opinion of themselves...Ever!"

(profound!)

So there's no point in asking them to. What needs to happen, is that they (and you) improve their opinion of themselves. This is so possible, it's NOT FUNNY and if you have been through one of my seminars, you'll know how powerful it can be.

My favourite story about changing peoples beliefs, was, I think, sent me by email as a true story, here it is anyway.

Seems this restaurant owner, who was one of the most positive people you could meet, was locking up his shop for the evening, when a robber came in the back door, and pointing a gun at him told him to give him the money from the safe. The owner was so frightened, he fumbled the keys, and couldn't get them to work, and in frustration, the gunman shot him, twice! The restaurant owner manages to call an ambulance, but as he is being taken from the ambulance, into the emergency area, he can see in the eyes of the staff, they don't think he will make it. Some nurse has been shouting at him "are you allergic to anything" but he can't speak. They wheel him into the operating area, and ask again "are you allergic to anything" over and over. He said at this point, he thought that if he was unable to let them know, he DID NOT WANT TO DIE, they wouldn't fight for him, so he gathered all of his strength, and as they asked him one last time...

"are you allergic to anything" he yelled... Bullets !!

He said at that point the whole room looked round, and everything seemed to speed up. You see their belief had changed, in that moment, from "he's gonna die" to

"we have a fighter"

If you call into his restaurant today and ask "how ya doin" you'll hear the reply " if I was any better I'd be twins" but if he hadn't changed their beliefs he'd be dead.

What are, at least, three things you would need to believe, to absolutely know this process will work for you.

<u>Write them down now:</u>

1.

2

3.

What are three strength's you have and
how do you know,

i.e: what evidence do you have
to support your belief

As a coach I ask lots of questions designed to discover peoples strengths during my first interview with a client. Questions like: what is the most challenging thing they have ever had to do? Their greatest success? Toughest day, and how did they overcome the difficulties? When the interview is over I always feed back some evidence of the strength I think they have demonstrated, and then the strength itself. If they decide to work with me as their coach I have a nice bank of strengths for the future. If they decide I'm not the coach for them I send them the whole list and wish them well.

You could ask yourself the same questions, and ask yourself what was the main strength you called upon to get yourself through. If you are able to improve your own (or your clients if you are coaching) self image even slightly you have just improved your likelihood of success many fold.

" People are like tea-bags they don't know their own strength until you put them in Hot water"

It's what I call Evidence based Strength centred feedback. Catch people doing things well and tell them.

That includes yourself !

So do the question and strength exercise for yourself.

1. _____
_____

2. _____
_____

3. _____
_____

Recap...

You should now have drawn your wheel, identified the areas that are important to you, worked out where you think you are against where you should be by today. You will have identified what 10 looks like or have a number of outcomes to work towards, listed in the next segments of the wheel, or second ring.

You should also have three beliefs which are burrowing away in your subconscious mind looking for support, and a number of strength centred stories from your past,

top job...

...well done, bit of a celebration I think

What do you Want

As a coach I have spoken to hundreds of individuals, as a trainer and speaker it's thousands, and I always ask what people want. Now if you have been kind enough to sit through one of my presentations, you'll know I speak to some pretty enlightened, smart people, and they don't know what they want either. And the ones who think they know what they want haven't got it yet , and when I ask why not, what I get is their <u>STORY.</u>

Now on occasion I say things which are profound, I'll print it in bold for you and warn you when it's coming so you don't miss it.

...psst this is profound

"The only reason people can't have what they want, is their story about why they can't have what they want "

Read that again.

What the wheel does is avoid story. The centre wheel is a snap shot of the areas that are important to you, in your life at this moment, and a measurement of how you feel about them. (i.e. reality)

The next wheel, or ring, is what you want, or what you want to achieve, (Goal) and you thought you didn't know... So there's a giant step right there.

You see if you can just stop the story, our subconscious mind is quite happy to tell us what we want. Cool aye?

I used to get all technical and explain how it works, but you're smart people, and you don't need to know how electricity works to switch on a light, do you?

When I interview smart people who are particularly good at something, they usually don't have a clue how they do what they do.

My greatest asset as a coach, is my unshakeable belief in the amazing ability of people, to have all the answers, to all of the problems they will ever come up against in their life, my belief in and how truly remarkable they can be.

Pssst, that includes you.

So trust yourself.

So when your relationships start to improve, your waistline shrinks, you've got more money left at the end of the month, more direction and drive or you're just plain happier. I'm sure you won't be upset, that you don't know how your subconscious enabled you to do it all.

Ok... Next, you guessed it draw another wheel outside the first two, this is when people run out of room, so I'll tell you now there will be one more wheel. While this book is a good place to start drawing your wheel, when you really get into this you may need a bigger piece of paper.

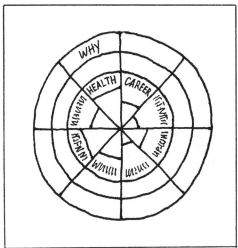

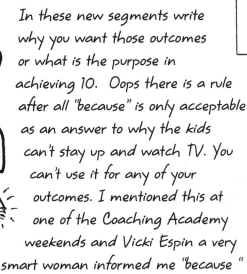

In these new segments write why you want those outcomes or what is the purpose in achieving 10. Oops there is a rule after all "because" is only acceptable as an answer to why the kids can't stay up and watch TV. You can't use it for any of your outcomes. I mentioned this at one of the Coaching Academy weekends and Vicki Espin a very smart woman informed me "because "

is a perfectly acceptable answer. She wouldn't tell me
what the acceptable question was though. I listened,
kept quiet, filed it for future reference, and went about
my business.

I'm no fool. I fight the fights
I can WIN.

So if you had a health area and you were a bit off track,
say.. 5 or 6 then 10 might have been a specific weight
with a good nutrition program, a sustainable, fun exercise
program, good skin. Plenty of sleep, can't wait to get up
in the morning bursting with energy, kinda thing.

"Why" might be, to keep up with my kids. To live
longer, in better condition. To be able to take
up a sport, or in today's multi tasking, stress
driven, got to be super mum or dad world ,
it might just be enough energy to go out
dancing Friday night instead of
collapsing in front of the
box when you stagger
home.

Actually she did
tell me later.

"WE all need to
BE at CAUSE if
we are to BE
in control of
our destiny"

Nice answer !

This segment of the wheel should also be completed fast, let the ideas flow, let them overflow if they are coming. It's fine if they spill out all over the page at this point, it's not a "neatest wins" competition. You can always do it again, in fact you will do this at least quarterly when you see how useful it can be.

Later I will show you how you can use this as a specific problem solving tool, a green light thinking tool, a tool to facilitate meetings, and a sales target/training analysis tool and lots more.

I'll also show you how to do it really fast.

Complete your "why, Purpose " part of the wheel now.

This is a great time for another recap, have a read through what you have created so far, if there are any areas that you can add an idea too, do that now, if things pop into your mind jot them down straight away. You know how when you are talking to someone and an idea pops to the surface of your mind, if you don't get it out 2 seconds later you're wondering what it was you were going to say. You will find that as your subconscious opens, and has more opportunity, and confidence, to pass you ideas, it will get better at it, and it will happen faster, it's like training a muscle, the harder you work it, the stronger it gets. But for now capture everything as it comes to you.

So take 15 to 20 minutes to review your wheel now

Now, on a separate piece of paper, or in your diary, or your journal, jot down how you _FEEL_ right now.

Do that before you read on.

Or as I said, use the Margins or Note pages provided

When people get to this point they often feel so much better, they have a huge rush of energy, a sense of purpose and direction, which is often a new experience, or at least one they haven't felt for a while. At this point I had a much better idea of where I was in my life. I had the beginnings of a picture and a feel for what I wanted, and had started to look at why I wanted it and why it was important to me. I was just so much further forward than I had been on any goals process before. The really great part was that for the first time it all felt connected, I felt congruent.

Interlude

Quotes

"There are persons so independent
that you cannot depend on them". (Anon)

Poise; Lifting the eyebrows instead of the roof. (Anon)

Great Coaching Tool

Tact is the ability to see others
as they see themselves. (Anon)

He who can take advice,
is sometimes superior
to he who can give it. (Anon)

The toughest form of mountain climbing
is climbing out of the rut. (Anon)

What are the facts ? Again and again and again – what
are the facts ? Shun wishful thinking, ignore divine
revelation, forget what "the stars foretell" avoid
opinion, care not what the neighbours think, never
mind the unguessable "verdict of history" – what are
the facts, and to how many decimal places ? You pilot
always into an unknown future ; facts are your single
clue. Always get the facts. (R.H)

Ego- something that enables people
to bear living with themselves. (Anon)

Keep your eyes open before marriage
and half closed afterwards. (Anon)

Whenever women have insisted on absolute equality
with men, they have invariably ended up with the dirty
end of the stick. What they are and what they can do
makes them superior to men, and their proper tactic is
to demand special privileges, all the traffic will bear
"equality" is a disaster.   (R.H)

The only people who like to be laughed at
usually get paid for it. (Anon)

A status symbol is anything you can't afford,
but did. (Anon)

A child is not a vase to be filled,
but a plant to be cultivated. (Anon)

The one thing that hurts more than paying income tax,
is not paying income tax. (Anon)

The man who cannot spare the time for a holiday
is not running his business properly. (Anon)

Never crowd youngsters about their private affairs –
sex especially. When they are growing up, they are
nerve ends all over, and resent (quite properly) any
invasion of their privacy. Oh sure they'll make
mistakes – but that's *their* business, not yours.

(You made your own mistakes, did you not ?) (R.H)

A hint suffices to a wise man. (Anon)

Failure is not defeat. It only comes from
getting a little experience. (Anon)

A human being should be able to change a diaper,
plan an invasion, butcher a hog, conn a ship, design a
building, write a sonnet, balance accounts, build a
wall, set a bone, comfort the dying, take orders, give
orders, cooperate, act alone, solve equations, analyse a
new problem, pitch manure, program a computer,
cook a tasty meal, fight efficiently, and die gallantly.

" Specialization is for insects." (R.H)

The proper way to think of business
is in terms of service. (R.H)

"If you're not fired with enthusiasm,
you will be fired, with enthusiasm". (N.J.R)

"People are like Teabags, they don't know their own
strength until you put them in hot water.
(*Elenor Rosvelt*)

"Always listen to experts, they'll tell you what
can't be done, and why. Then do it. (R.H)

Everything in excess! To enjoy the flavour of life,
take big bites. Moderation is for monks. (R.H)

Throughout history, poverty is the normal condition of
man. Advances which permit this norm to be
exceeded – here and there, now and then – are the
work of an extremely small minority, frequently
despised, often condemned and almost always
opposed by all
right-thinking people. Whenever this tiny minority is
kept from creating, or (as sometimes happens) is
driven out of a society, the people then slip back into
abject poverty.

This is known as "bad luck" (R.H)
Just when you think you can make ends meet at last,
someone moves the ends. (Anon)

"A wise man knows everything;
a shrewd one, everybody". (Anon)

Dear, don't bore him with trivia or burden him with
your past mistakes. The happiest way to deal with a
man is never to tell him anything he does not need to
know. (R.H)

There are times when silence
can be more musical than any song.

The correct way to punctuate a sentence that starts:
"Of course it's none of my business but - is to place a
period after the word "but." Don't use excessive force
in supplying such a moron with a period. Cutting his
throat is only a momentary pleasure and is bound to
get you talked about. (R.H)

"All's fair in love and war" –
what a contemptible lie ! (R.H)

Don't try and have the last word.

You might get it. (R.H)
Sin lies only in hurting other people. All other "sins"
are invented nonsense. (Hurting yourself is not sinful
– just stupid.) (R.H)

"I came, I saw, she conquered."
(The original Latin seems to have been garbled.)
(R.H)

A committee is a life form with six or
more legs and no brain. (R.H)

"A new computer
should come with a free 7 year old".
(C.J.R)

Before borrowing money from a friend,
decide which you need the most. (Anon)

" Everybody lies about sex". (R.H)

*(R.H) - Robert Heinlein
*(N.J.R) - Nic Rixon
*(C.J.R) - C.J. Rixon, My father

Decisions, decisions, decisions !

Now the wheel so far has all been about seeking, looking within to find the answer to the question that caused you to pick up this book in the first place, the 64 thousand dollar question.

What do you want, and how do you get it..., well you probably have a much clearer picture now, and isn't that cool !

So what next ?
Guess what... Yep...
Draw another wheel.
This is the last one I promise.

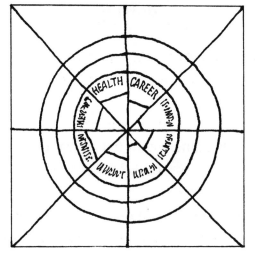

Actually, I've changed my mind, just extend the lines all the way to the edge of the page —
(The Seeker strikes again!)

Action

In this final segment write at least one or more action, you can and will take within 24 hours, that will move you closer to your outcome, or closer to 10

Remember all the work so far will have been wasted if you stop now, again if the action ideas start to flow capture them all, don't judge them at this stage just let them flow. They don't all have to be something you can do within 24 hours but there should be at least one thing you can do within that time period. You can review and prioritise later.

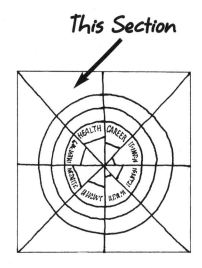

This Section

Take no more than 30 to 40 minutes to complete this section

Complete your final wheel section now.

I find that most of my clients can get quite a good wheel with lots of information on it and plenty of action ideas in 2 to 3 hours. The participants on the coaching weekend get just an introduction to this process and 80% + get extra clarity and direction in just 2 hours.

(you have the whole process and all the time you need)

If you are doing this for yourself and you are finding it difficult to come up with action ideas, you may need to go back and look at the wheel inside this one, the WHY and the PURPOSE may not be powerful enough.
(Ditto for your clients if you're coaching)

Most people who know anything about goal setting will tell you "WHY" is 90% of the equation, and how is 10%.

Kids know this.
"You've got to go to bed now" "Why!" "Because"

Think about it, your spouse tells you they need you to get up at 4.00am tomorrow morning, what's your first question ?... Absolutely... why?

"Because we're going to the Bahamas" " No problem, I'll just set the alarm"

You see HOW to get up isn't really that difficult, is it.

Now you're sitting there asking yourself, how did this ordinary bloke get me to do all that in just a few hours. Well apart from my total belief in your ability, I heard a great analogy recently which I thought did a great job of explaining how we did it, you and I .

This may not apply to you, but most people find sorting out their finances a bit of a challenge. Peps, issas, mortgages, investments, tax, pensions, etc, etc. It's enough to drive you crazy. So they visit a financial advisor, who says "this is easy" because he has a whole bag of tools to calculate your risk ratio, the final figure for your endowment policy, the monthly contribution at a given rate of growth to arrive at a final figure at retirement, to cover the projected cost of your future life style.

phew !

They take your "mess" and arrange it into a neat list of "as is" "outcomes" and "actions" result ?

"One happy client"

The wheel is just that, a contextual tool, which speaks to your subconscious mind, to enable you to reorganise your thoughts, into... Where are you now, what do you want, why do you want it, and what are you prepared to do to get it.

Cool hmm !

Talking it through.

There is one final, but vital part to the wheel exercise, that you need to complete, before we move on. I can not emphasize the importance of this enough, so I won't, just trust me and do it!

Find a good friend, one you trust to be non judgmental. Ask them if they will listen to you. You can tell them what you are doing if you want, it shouldn't effect the quality of the silence. Tell them you don't want any feed back or advice, you just want them to listen, while you talk through some ideas out loud. You will have to trust me that what you say will sound different when you say it out loud to a real person.

By a show of hands at the coaching weekends I get 50% + who say that, as they were talking about their wheel out loud, either the problem didn't sound as bad as they had thought it was, or the solution just popped into their head, or a particular course of action presented itself, almost as if it had come from outside...

...Like I say trust me and do it.

Tell your listener that even if you stop speaking they should not say anything, no comment, no interruption. They should give you at least 5 min where only you speak. You should set yourself a timer for 5 min total to talk through the whole wheel experience, because when you know you are under time pressure your subconscious mind will give you the important stuff you need to review first.

If you think you have run out of things to say, you will often find your mind is just sorting, deciding what to say next.

Now most of the time you never get the chance, to continue with your train of thought, because who ever you are talking to interrupts with a question, or starts to tell you their story. (Take Note's Coaches)

So keep focussing on your wheel, keep reading it in your mind, keep processing, and just say whatever comes into your head. NOW you know why you need someone you trust, they need to be comfortable with long silences, and confidential information.

Do this exercise before you move onto the next stage.

If you're a coach looking to develop this as a tool to use when coaching I can not stress strongly enough how important it is to get comfortable with leaving your clients to process their thoughts, I always say that if you coach by phone, and your client asks "are you still there" then you've given them enough time.

So do this for yourself, so you can experience the power
of giving your subconscious mind space to think.
One of the Coaching Academy graduates
phrased it beautifully.

"Listening while coaching creates
a pool of silence, people
just have to dive in"

SSSSH!

So do it before you read on.

If you've now done this for yourself you will understand
the power of wandering around unmolested in your
own mind.

If you haven't, go
do it now !!!

MY MIND

Motivation

If you're about to read on and you haven't done the "sharing your thoughts out loud" with some one who will listen because you're a little embarrassed or scared here's a little story for you from Zig Ziglar.

There was this rich Texan, and he had a beautiful daughter who was his only heir. He had oil wells, he had land, and he had cattle. Now on her 21st birthday he had a big party and invited all the eligible bachelors in the area for a group prospecting party. Around midnight he invited them all out by the pool, which he had had the foresight to stock with alligators and poisonous snakes.

"If one of you will jump in and swim the length of this pool, you can have the choice of my daughters hand in marriage, and I don't need to tell you she's my only heir and will one day inherit all my wealth, or you can have my best oil well, or 100,000 head of my best cattle".

Almost before he finished speaking, there was a splash at one end of the pool, followed, almost immediately, by the emergence of a dripping wet young man at the other end. The rich Texan is amazed, "young man, you've just set a new world record for the 50 meter dash, I take it you want the hand of my daughter"

"No...Sir!"

"Well you don't look big enough to be a cattle man, so I take it it's the oil well" **"No...Sir!"**

"ok... cattle it is then" **"No...Sir!"**

"Well young man what on earth 'DO' you want"

"I want the name of the dude that pushed me in the swimming pool"

Some times the challenges we face look as scary as hell, but if someone will just give us a little push, once we're in the water, it's not too bad. So take the plunge, dive into the silence.

phone a friend.

Now I can't know how you feel or felt when you finished your wheel and talked it through with someone else, but I bet I can get close. I've taken thousands of people through this exercise, and reactions and feed back vary. Some people are stunned at how much they were able to capture, they feel euphoric and have a new sense of direction and purpose.

Some have ideas and solutions to problems that have plagued them for years, and the solutions just popped into their mind during the process. Others are amazed at what they've written and as they talk it through with someone else, can't believe it, as they hear themselves solving their own problems.

I usually stand there with this big "I told you so" grin on my face.

"Man... I wish people believed in themselves as much as I do"

" Believe in <u>THEM</u> I mean "

So let me ask you, did you gain a little more clarity on where you are in your life right now ?

Do you have a clearer idea of what you want and, do you know some of the things you need to do to get it ?

So here's the question, are you ready?... apart from the wheel, how much did I add to your thought process ?...

How much did the person who listened to you add ?...

The answer to both of those questions should be......

(NOTHING   )

Which means, oops, you did it all on your own, Way t' go !

It is an amazing thing, the subconscious mind, probably the most powerful goal achieving tool in existence. And yours is now switched on and waiting for instructions.

Glass half full

We need to be careful now, as your mind doesn't know the difference between having some thing in your life and not having something.

Let me explain by giving you an example.

Have you ever had someone call you, or start a conversation with the words, "Don't Worry".... what's the first thing you did ?

Not only did you start worrying, you started making up stuff to worry about, you made pictures in your head of people you know, in all sorts of terrible situations. Then they say, "<u>Calm</u> <u>down</u>, <u>Calm</u> <u>down</u>, I said Don't Worry"

Make a picture in your head right now of not eating a delicious fresh cream cake or chocolate, or don't make a picture of your favourite food, and what pops into your head ?, that's right!, all the stuff I said don't think of. Gives a new meaning to "don't get run over" doesn't it. Or "don't spill this it's hot" you can see it happening in your head can't you?

66

That's why, you'll notice, people who can tell you what they DON'T WANT, usually got a whole bunch of what they don't want in their lives.

P.S. "That was profound"

So during this next part it's important to focus on what you want, not what you don't want.
With what we've done with the wheel so far, you should now have a good idea of what's IMPORTANT to you. This next process will find out what you WANT. What some of your gaols are, what do you want to do, who do you want to be.

Time out for a moment. As I was writing this section this morning the phone rang and one of my favourite clients/friends was on the phone, one smart woman, her exact words were: "I'm driving to a meeting this morning, and I want to make sure I don't get all emotional and cry" now what do you think she was closest to. We had a ten minute (reprogram her brain) session to build a list of what she wanted, and how she wanted to be, and how she saw the person she was going to meet.

Now in about 2 hours time I'll tell you how she got on.

What do you want... Part 2

1st rule is, oh yeah, there are no rules, and I really mean there are no rules, no limits no matter how far fetched or unlikely the idea or thing might be, if it pops into your head write it down.

Take a fresh piece of paper mix it with your favourite pen and a quiet hour of undisturbed time, add a comfortable chair and your favourite CD and write down your dream list.

Everything you would like to do before the rocking chair and blanket. Every thing you would like to have, the complete life style, get it all down on paper. And finally everything you would like to be. (be taller is tough, not impossible, but tough) being the right height for your weight is much easier.

(yeah, I know, you need to think about the height, weight thing)

Before you start, let me help you, by putting your mind at rest. When I first did this I wanted everything and I thought it will take me forever to write it all down, now I did end up with quite a list, but I was still running out of things to put on the list after about 20 minutes. So give yourself a nice quiet hour and keep writing, don't judge anything, the crazier it gets the better, all you are doing is giving your subconscious mind permission to look in the dustiest corners of your mind, for all your "stuff" This is usually where people store their most passionate dreams, they hide them there to stop other people from stealing them, or crushing them. Reject nothing, as your mind is also a generalisation device, if you tell it 'I don't think I want that or can't do that or become that, it will gather all of the other thoughts and dreams that are similar and leave them in your subconscious.

So go mad, dream a little.

Today _____ I designed my Life

Do it NOW

Dream Sheet

Dream Sheet

Now if you finished your list, leave it for 24 hours, and during that time keep a note pad or Dictaphone with you and jot down all the other stuff (technical term for goal setting, "stuff") that pops out of your mind. If it takes a couple of days before we're back together that's fine. Keep your note book handy, add, add, add.

Welcome back, that's quite an exercise isn't it?
If you haven't added all your new stuff to your original list, do that now... phew !

When I finished my list, as well as having a feeling of accomplishment, I thought "how on earth am I ever gona get all that" Now if you haven't got 5 pages of stuff, that's ok. I've seen every length of list from Mr Enlightened, who had one thing. "Be happy"

To my daughter's Christmas list which also only had one thing "Harrods"

However if you've got a bunch of stuff and there's a lot of it, here's what you do.

For each goal, answer the following question, in one sentence. Why do you want it? Work through the whole list. If you're struggling to find the answer to one of your goals, put it to one side for now and move on. You should end up with a slightly shorter list, as long as you didn't use "Because" as one of the answers. If you can answer why to everything on the list, it all stays.

If you have arrived at this point in the book, and done all the work, then congratulations, you now form part of a very elite group of people who have taken the time to design their lives rather than just drift with the flow, because 10 years from now you will surely arrive, somewhere, the question is... Where ! and now is the time to design the next 10 years, and decide your destination.

When you get to the end of this book make sure where you've got to is not just the end of this book, but the end of a journey of discovery. In fact if you haven't done the work stop now, don't read any more, go back and do the work. Whatever reason you picked the book up for go back and do the exercises, trust me, it will make the investment you made in this book the best you ever made. For those of you who have done all the work so far, you have an inkling of why I'm asking them to do it. If you have done this with me in one of my seminars or been coached using my version of the wheel, you know!

If you haven't you'll never know...
... unless you do it.

I'd like one last shot at encouraging the last few who haven't started the process with me yet, forgive me if you have, you'll like the story anyway.

This happened during the process of editing this book.

I was doing a Wheel, Goals and motivation day and one of the participants was slightly distressed that she was unable to make a decision about what she wanted. Most of the people in the room had done the short wheel session with me during the course of the previous year, so I asked her how she had got on when she had done the short session.

"Oh" she said "I was too upset to do it"
She was still, visibly quite upset, but I said
"you need to do this exercise, so you'll
have your answer"

Well there were 45 or so people in the room and I touched base with Beverley several times during the day, and she seemed to be doing ok.
At the end of the day she came up to thank me for the day, and said she had made some progress. I gave her a gentle hug and sent my thoughts with her.

The next day I received this email

Dear Nic,

I need to tell you that I feel I have been affected at a deep level by the day we spent with you. I guess I must have been at the right level to accept what you were saying. It has made a real difference.

I have been really down for a while, and feeling very fragile. But something shifted yesterday. I look forward to your book!

Just doing the wheel yesterday I realised I am not ready to go back to SA and maybe I never will be. My priority is to become the best life-coach, add value to people's lives (and to my own). I want to become financially independent so any decision I make is from wholeness and not need.

Maybe one day you can give me a coaching session, then I will fly along! My first thought was,... could never afford you... Second thought was well sometimes quality is worth it for the difference it can make to the rest of my life!

Will send you a poem from a children's poetry book, was my daughter's favourite when she was 5 or 6 and now she is 20.

"I had a jar with a butterfly
I opened the lid and it flew to the sky
and these are things inside my head
waiting to be thought or said

Dreams and hopes and wonderings are
locked inside like a butterfly jar

Then when I feel safe and can be me
I can open the lid and set them free".

My vision is to have a cottage by the sea, somewhere beautiful where I feel safe. I can walk with my dogs, I will have two. I will run my life-coach practice from home, and I will write. (I have already taken the first step and sent an article off to various magazines). My home will reflect me and be my sanctuary.

Once I have done the wheel by myself, I will let you know. I certainly am going to tell Jonathan how valuable yesterday was.

On the actual residential weekend. You had two hours to pack in when essentially we needed one day, which we now have had!! It was too much to take in on the residential weekend.

Must add I had only had 3 hours sleep on Saturday night, just due to my thoughts going around and around, so the fact that I was able to take in and participate as much as I did shows, ... either you are really fantastic, and/or I was really keen, and/or I was taking it in by osmosis!! However main thing is that I took it in and assimilated it, and suddenly my life and the world makes sense. So talk about adding value!! If this sounds like gushing, well my life has been changed and it feels like a whole new day... and I have feelings of enthusiasm and passion for my life, and yes I can get there...

Its always been there.. but too much fear, anxiety, doubt. Coming to London has freed me to truly listen. You may not know it but back home in SA, I would not have commented and asked questions like I did on Sunday. I would never have sat in the front row... So thank you.

Best regards

Beverly Bernhardt

So if you have done all the work, fantastic
Less than 10 % of the population ever get this far.
Maybe that accounts for the figure I heard recently,
that over 85 % of us are unhappy in our work.

So.... I got this far and........

"One thought, if you are a coach, is the Client always blames you for <u>THEIR</u> success".

I Still didn't get what I wanted !! I'd written it down,
stated it in the positive, had pictures of it on my wall,
put a date on it, and it still didn't show up.

"SO WHAT THE HELL HAVE I DONE ALL THIS FOR ?"

Ok I hear you, calm down. The next part is the pivot on
which my whole world changed. This turbo charged
every area of my life. This is the part that has people
sitting in stunned silence at the seminars, the next part
is what happened to Beverly,... but hey you've done a lot
of work, you must be tired, why don't we take a break
and finish off tomorrow, wadaya say,

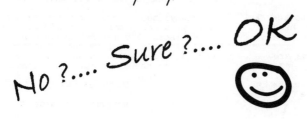

No ?.... Sure ?.... OK
☺

Alignment

This is where you match what you want with what's important to you.

You will need your wheel and your dream list.

Take your first goal, and your wheel, and measure the goal against the wheel to see which areas it improves and which it doesn't. For example, one of my goals was a new house. The areas of my wheel and how they were affected were;

Health	no	Fun	no
Wealth	no	Social life	yes
Family	yes	Friends	yes
Career	no	Knowledge	no
Spirituality	no	Contribution	no

So buying a new house, for me, scored 3/8 of course there are a number of factors that could change the score, If I built it myself then Health and Wealth may have scored yes. If we moved away from our friends to a remote area Friends and Social may have been No.

Each wheel and goal comparison is for you to make your own judgments with. Here's a tip though, if you find yourself working too hard to convince yourself one way or the other, you're probably deluding yourself. The other comment people make is that some areas on the wheel are more important than others. If it's your wheel and you think that, then they are, just give different values to the areas.

The Health section might have a value of 3. Your Fun section might score 1. So what ever your goal from your dream list, is if it improves both Health and Fun, with the values as above (3 & 1) your score would be at least 4. If you're healthy and miserable and bored though, it might be the other way round. Go with your gut feeling and don't get too hung up on values.

Go ahead and mark all of your goals against the wheel now.

" Hey I never said this would be easy, "

but it will turbo charge your life, so do it before you read any further" "actually, read this next bit first, then do it"

When I'm coaching a new client, I take them through this whole process. It usually takes up the first two or three sessions. I often set it as home work and we discuss it next time we meet, even if it's on the phone, they can still talk me through it. So, if you take two to three weeks to do this, that's ok. I would say that the faster you can do it the more momentum you create, but some people like to enjoy the process of discovery, there can be quite a lot of emotion the first time you do this properly, so in your own time, after all, I'm here any time you open the book, and you will get faster the more you use it.

Note for coaches....

The 1st session I do with a client, is free, I just talk about the client, get to know them. I'm focussed on discovering their strengths, as I said, so I always look for challenges they have overcome, the things they have done and do.

If we have rapport and they want to go ahead, and they have convinced me they really want to move forward, I give them the wheel to start things moving.

I ask them to fill in the first three sections and when we meet next, they talk through the process. We work through the ACTION steps in the coaching session.

So as you can see the session has great power because they are already sold. They have all their reality, what they want, and why, written down. Getting them into action is so much easier when they are at this stage. The other surprise, is that what they pick to work on, is seldom what they came to me with in the first place.

Home work from this session is the dream list up to the why question, we do the comparison with the wheel during the next coaching session. I always want to be a part of that as there is so much power and emotion in the process and I want to help them harness it and use it

Now you can mark your goals against the wheel.

When you've finished marking all of your goals against the wheel and each goal has a score of X out a maximum of the number of areas on your wheel come back and we'll move on to the next part.

Well I'm interested to find out if we had a similar experience. Did you find some strange scores?
I found that the top three goals I had on my list, the ones I thought were the most important scored 1 or 0 and the "after thought" things, some of the things that hadn't come out until the next day were scoring 7 and above.

If your scores are anything like mine you're probably as stunned as I was. The realisation that I had been focused on working for stuff, that wasn't really important to me. This is probably why I wasn't really putting in a 100 % effort, and why I kept failing to reach my goals.

Someone once said to me that

"Goals didn't work for them"

Well in my case what I discovered was, that "I didn't work for my goals" What happened, when I finally got my goals, in alignment with my wheel, - with what was really important to me, was nothing short of miraculous.

Now don't beat yourself up if, like me , you've been chasing the wrong stuff, because most of the people I have done this with have the same experience, and in just a moment I will tell you the really great part about this.

First lets have a look at how far out my list was. Jot down what you think may have been on one of my first lists back when I was a 27 year old enthusiastic ambitious young man, just making his way in the world.

1.
- -

2
- -

3.
- -

Answers on page.....96

Ok did you get close. Transparent ay....,
boys and their toys. So now the confession 15th on my
list was "BE A GREAT DAD", followed very quickly
(with the hope that Linda would never see) was,..
"BE A GREAT HUSBAND". You see at 27 I was a
married man with two kids. I had spent the first 4
years of their life, chasing the "car, money, house", life
style, Things that I thought were important, because I
didn't know what really mattered.

Or rather I didn't know I knew.

Let's check out, how two of my goals scored against my
wheel. The car for me was a 911 sc coupe, it had been
on my list since I was 14. For me it was the ultimate
sign of success, and after all it was the eighties.
Fifteenth on my list was "be a great dad"
So car against the wheel,
HEALTH,   Don't think so.
WEALTH,   Not a chance.
FAMILY,   Nope.
CAREER, not in the business I was in, you
pull up in a car like that, my customers
would all be checking their prices.
SPIRITUALITY,   No.

FUN, ...Oh Yes.

SOCIAL LIFE naa (see friends) FRIENDS, the sort of friends a married man with two kids should have, nope. KNOWLEDGE / GROWTH, about owning a Porsche, possibly. About life, myself, my family and business, not a chance. And finally CONTRIBUTION to my fellow man, well unless I gave my fellow man a lift in the Porsche, no hope there either.

Score 1/10

Lets check out, "be a great dad"

HEALTH, if you got em you know how fit you have to be just to keep up, Yep. WEALTH, it's amazing how hard you will work for something important, and we are teaching both our kids to be smart investors so they'll be able to afford to keep us in the style to which we will become accustomed, yep. FAMILY, no brainer, yep. CAREER , see wealth, yep. SPIRITUALITY, I can not tell how moved and delighted I was to be voted coolest dad by my daughter's school friends, yep. FUN, yep. SOCIAL LIFE, school barbies, sports days, plays, speech days, our friends today are people we met through the kids and the schools, yep. FRIENDS, see "Social life"

KNOWLEDGE / GROWTH, massive, and never ending, yep. CONTRIBUTION to my fellow man, well I got involved in personal development to help me develop my kids. The first piece of material I ever read was called "Father Forgets" It was written by W Livingston Larned and was re printed in the Dale Carnegie book "How to win friends and influence people". Since reading that first piece, I have applied every thing I have learned to myself first, my family and business second, and more than 10,000 people so far, third. As Jethro would say 'I am doin' my best" but I'll let you decide on the contribution front.

Score 10/10

As "Father Forgets" had such a profound effect on me I have included it here.

Father Forgets

Listen, son: I am saying this as you lie asleep, one little paw crumpled under your cheek and the blond curls stickily wet on your damp forehead. I have stolen into your room alone. Just a few minutes ago, as I sat reading my paper in the library, a stifling wave of remorse swept over me.

Guiltily I came to your bedside.

There are things I was thinking, son: I had been cross to you. I had scolded you as you were dressing for school because you gave your face merely a dab with the towel. I took you to task for not cleaning your shoes. I called out angrily when you threw some of your things on the floor.

At breakfast I found fault too. You spilled things. You gulped down your food. You put your elbows on the table. You spread butter too thick on your bread. And as you started off to play and I made for my train, you turned and waved a hand and called out "Goodbye, Daddy!" and I frowned and said in reply, "Hold your shoulders back!"

Then it began all over again in the late afternoon. As I came up the road I spied you, down on your knees, playing marbles. There were holes in your socks. I humiliated you before friends by marching you ahead of me to the house. Socks were expensive—and if you had to buy them you would be more careful! Imagine that, son, from a father!

Do you remember later ,when I was reading in the library, how you came in timidly, with that hurt look in your eyes? When I glanced up over my paper, impatient at the interruption, you hesitated at the door. "What is it you want?" I snapped.

You said nothing, but ran across in one tempestuous plunge, and threw your arms around my neck and kissed me, and your small arms tightened with an affection that God had set blooming in your heart, and which even neglect could not wither. And then you were gone, pattering up the stairs.

Well, son, it was shortly afterwards that my paper slipped from my hands and a terrible sickening fear came over me. What has habit been doing to me? The habit of finding fault, of reprimanding—this was my reward to you for being a boy. It was not that I did not love you; it was that I expected too much of youth. I was measuring you by the yard stick of my own years.

And there was so much that was good and fine and true in your character. The little heart of you was as big as the dawn itself over the wide hills. This was shown by your spontaneous impulse to rush in and kiss me good night. Nothing else matters tonight, son. I have come to your bed-side in the darkness, and have knelt there ashamed!

It is a feeble atonement; I know you would not understand these things if I told them to you during your waking hours. But tomorrow I will be a real daddy! I will chum with you, and suffer when you suffer, and laugh when you laugh. I will bite my tongue when impatient words come. I will keep saying as if it is a ritual: He is nothing but a little boy - a little boy!"

I am afraid I have visualised you as a man. Yet as I see you now, son, crumpled and weary in your cot, I see that you are still a baby. Yesterday you were still in your mother's arms, your head on her shoulder.

I have asked too much, too much.

I read that piece sitting in an office on my own just after we had discovered our son was dyslexic. All the times I had asked if he was being lazy or stupid crashed down on me, and as I sat in that office, I literally broke down and sobbed like a kid, that soul wrenching crying that has you breathing in three times in every word, my heart just broke. and I sobbed. I tried to call Linda on the phone, to read it to her, but my throat closed and I couldn't speak. It took me years to be able to read that piece out loud, fortunately one of my main goals was "Be a great dad" I finally managed to read it out loud in 2002.

Back to your wheel experience

Now you may have had a totally different experience to mine, when you marked your wheel, and that's fine. The very point of this tool, is it is a, tailored tool and process, for the individual.

As I've already said, I found that most of the goals that had been top of my list, and therefore at the front of my mind, scored very low, two, one or nothing. The goals which came out later in the listing process, some that didn't arrive until the next day, goals and desires buried deep in my subconscious, were the ones that scored well. My decision, as I couldn't have it all right then, (and you need to make your own decision about this) was only to work on goals that scored 6 or more, which was less than a third of the goals on my list.

Now I don't know if you remember the "great news" I promised you back on page........ Well here it is. When I got focused on what was really important to me, and put all my effort into working towards that, all the other stuff showed up as well.

The reason I got voted coolest dad, by my daughters friends, was for picking her up from school on a custom Harley Davidson motorbike.

I'd like to think it was for treating her and her friends like adults, and listening to them as well, but I think the Harley helped.

When I'd been trying to work for it, (the stuff, that is) I couldn't stay motivated, but when my focus changed, when my goals were in alignment with what was really important to me, my life exploded, and the joy and passion I have in my life today are due to that one distinction. I had no problem getting up early, working hard, and efficiently so I could get home at a reasonable time, to have time for the family. Once I understood that they were what was really important. The harder and smarter I worked the more time I had, and I had a whole bunch of extra time because my goals list had been reduced by 2/3rds and the more time I had, the more fun I had and the more time I had, to learn to do it better, and round and round.

I only do what I love now, and so will you.

Wow you've done a lot ! I would like to congratulate you... and thank you for allowing me to be part of this process with you, but we ain't finished yet. My second distinction or observation was, success required seekers who took action. Well now you have to take all this information and integrate it into your daily plan for living your life. But before I show you how to do that, here's a challenge: make room for a little magic, design in magic moments for yourself and your friends and family.

I'd like to share two of mine with you if you'll allow.

Linda and I had gone to Hawaii to a financial investment / personal development seminar. A bit more inspiring than Gravesend, and there was a particular exercise we had to complete, that involved a physical challenge, to demonstrate supporting each other. It involved both of us scaling a 50 foot pole and climbing out onto wires attached to the pole. These were connected to two other poles that were 30 feet away and 20 feet apart, so as our wires left our pole they widened from nothing to 20 foot apart.

Got the picture, good.

Now I don't do heights so Linda had to supply loads of encouragement, to get me off the ground. She went up first and talked me up every inch of the way. She climbed out onto her wire no problem and eventually got me out onto mine. We were linked to a safety harness, but

my brain was in rebellion overdrive, and there was no
way I could have done it without her. The idea then was
to clasp each others hands above our heads, lean in on
one another forming an arch between the two wires,
and start to move along them getting further apart at
our feet, whilst still holding hands.
The point of the exercise being to show that we would
have to both lean on each other and support each other,
and that no matter how big the difference in size and
strength, each partner was necessary for there to be
balance in the relationship.
So there we were on our wires, her left hand in my
right, both our other hands holding on to the pole. We
slowly move along the wire until we're about 18 inches
apart, and 4 feet from the pole, the sun is just setting,
our team of about 25 people are on the ground, shouting
encouragement, along with hundreds of others.
You couldn't have written a script better than this.
Linda looks up into my eyes, bursts into tears, and with
them streaming down her face says "I love you so
much, I would never be here if it wasn't for you." So, I
burst into tears as well, and she looks at me, and in total
trust, that I will follow her lets go of the pole, and takes
a step along the wire. With total trust that she will hold
me up, I let go and we clasp each others hands and
get our balance.

There we are 50 feet in the air, the sun is almost gone, the ocean is on fire, the people on the ground are going crazy. We're holding each others hands, supporting each other, laughing and crying our hearts out, moving slowly along the wire one careful step at a time, looking into each other, (no I didn't type that wrong) physically moving apart, emotionally growing stronger and closer until I thought I would burst with the sheer joy of it. Finally we couldn't go any further and as one we stepped off the wire, grabbed each other and were lowered into the cheering crowd.

Create magic moments...
Draw a wheel...
Dream a little...

Magic Moments ....
...for the price of a phone call.

I remember one of the cheapest magic moment ever.
We used to live way out in the country, which was at
least one and a half to two hours journey from my office,
so I was late home quite a lot before I got my act
together.

On this particular night I left early and got
home about 7.00pm I switched off the car
lights, it was dark, and quietly crept up the
drive. I managed to get in the house and
up the stairs without Linda hearing me. I
then get on my mobile phone and phone
home, I pretend I am still at work, and ask if
she (Linda) will pop upstairs to get a
file I need, which is in the bedroom.
Thinking I'm still at work, she figures I'm not
going to be home before 9.00pm at least, so with a big
huff, she goes off to the bedroom to
get the file.

CREEP CREEP!

I'll let you finish the story....

Magic Moments ....
...for the price of a phone call.

Fifteen years later, my daughter is on an evening course in London, for public speaking and life skills. She and I had spent some time preparing this particular nights presentation, as I knew she had been quite nervous.

Em's always phoned when she got out of the course, just before she got on to the tube. So I ask "how'd it go" most unusually she was very non committal "awright" So I try again "So what happened then" "yeah, it wasn't too bad" so I hang up and I'm ashamed to admit it said "I don't know why I bother trying to talk to that girl" I know what you're thinking, but hey! Feet of clay and all that.

Forty five minutes later Em's comes bounding through the front door screaming

"I GOT TWO AWARDS"
"I WON _TWO_" "I WON _TWO_"

Oops, busted.
You're kids pick up all your good habits too.

Magic moments you remember for a life time, for the cost of a phone call.

What goes around comes around.

So make time for the magic moments, and remember they don't create themselves.

Putting it all into action.... or
"I love it when a plan comes together"

Now this part does take some discipline, and some time. It helps if you have a good coach in the first few months, whilst this becomes a habit, but here's what you do. As much as I hate em, and I'll tell you why later, make a to-do list. Jot down every thing you may have to, or should do, next week. You do this some time over the week end. Make sure you have your week end to-do list as well. Then have a look at your high scoring goals, and pick between 4 and 6 to work on that week, the ones which most match your activity, and your personal circumstances, for that week. They may also be the ones that will affect the area of your wheel you most need to take action in.

Some of your goals will be ongoing, some short term, some long term, and some may not be relevant at this time. You can break the long term ones down into a series of short steps, which you then plan around your own personal time table, but make sure you schedule them in. As you look at the items on your goal list and your to do list, note how much is activity focused and how much is outcome or results focused.

Answers from Page.....82

1. MONEY - Make a Mint.
2. CAR - 911 Porsche.
3. HOUSE - Designed & built for us.

Help list for Page.....28

Health	Fun	Wealth
Social Life	Growth	Career
Learning	Family	Knowledge
Friends	Location	Spirituality
Contribution		

Don't get hung up on activity, make sure all planning is based around, and designed to achieve, the outcomes you want.

For example don't put call my dad, or mum, or sister. Describe the outcome you want as a result of making the call. Let my dad, mum, sister know how much I care about them, that I love em and was thinking of them. Or call Fred and ask for the business.
Then check how many other things on your to do list would fit into the outcome, "connect with my family, let them know I care" and you add those to-do's to the list of actions you would be prepared to take to achieve your outcome.

You then move on to the next free item on your to-do list Redefine it as an outcome, check through your to-do list and gather any other to-do items which could fall into that outcome. You work through your to-do's until you have converted them all to outcomes and grouped those that fall into the same category or area of your wheel. It is much easier to focus on 6 or 7 outcomes, than on a to-do list with 25 things on.

I know this seems complicated to start with, and I could have provided you with all sorts of pre-drawn work sheets, but they don't allow you to freeform it to suit your style. Some people, draw pictures, you may be a mind mapper, I've just learnt a great colour coded system that is brilliant and simple. **(Watch this space)**

Well, not this one,
but you know what I mean

So whether you are doing this for yourself, or using it as a tool to coach someone else, (in which case, of course, you should have, half a dozen ways of using it for yourself anyway)

Here is my quick way.

Check your wheel, which areas stand out as the ones you should be working on right now, start with 3 or 4 What are your outcomes for the following week for the areas you have picked, write them down. What are your to-do's for the week, group the ones that fit the areas of your wheel. Delete any that don't have to be done next week, and make sure any left have a result / outcome focus.

Done !

You should now really only have 4 areas to focus on for the week.

What this does, is tells your subconscious mind what to focus on, so that when an opportunity pops up that would fit the criteria of moving you forward in one of your focus areas, you are made aware of it, and can then seize the moment.

What happens when you have a great long to do list, is you are too busy ticking off things on your list to notice the opportunity when it smacks you in the face.

Example...

I had a "family focus" week, and my outcome was to contact my close family, and let them know how I felt about them, (I don't mean, piece of my mind, type stuff) I mean how much I care about them. So I had this whole list of actions I was prepared to take. Mothers day card. Send my dad some cardboard picture carrying packs for his paintings. Call my sister, ask how her new job is going, and just listen. Etc etc.

Tuesday of that week, I had dropped into our local bathroom showroom, to pick up some small item for our own bathroom. The staff were pulling out one of the displays. It had one of these super, soak you from every angle, shower panels, that usually cost a fortune, knocked down to about 40 %.

My parents were just having a new bathroom put in, and had not yet ordered a shower. So I bought it, put it in the car and drove it down to their home in Wiltshire, I took Linda with me, and as per our usual way of announcing our arrival didn't phone until I was sitting on their drive way. So big surprise, lots of hugs, they were delighted to see us, and were delighted with the shower, and the added bonus was my sister was visiting as well and we got to have a nice long chat, as we hadn't seen each other for a while. We took them out to dinner that night, and all in all, had a super day. My mum phoned the next day and said that neither of them could remember having had such a super day for a long long time.

Now, if I was to-do list focused, I might have popped into the bathroom shop, and out again, in my hurry to get back to my to-do list, and missed a wonderful opportunity.

Who knows ?

Why I don't like To - Do Lists.

Think of it this way, can you ever finish a to-do list?

Answer ? No.

Could you do all the things on your to-do list
and not accomplish anything?

Answer ? "Of course!"

Because so many people (not us of course) confuse
activity with accomplishment.

An Autumn Moment

One of those Ripe fruit gathering moments, where the sowing of the seed, the constant watering and feeding, the weeding and pruning, all came together in a short car journey.

A friend of ours and his son had joined Oly and I to go roller blading in Hyde Park. I had my special "I'm here to embarrass my children" tee-shirt on, and we were making our way up through London, in no particular hurry, and Oly's friend turns to him and asks "do you get pocket money" so he replies "Yep"
"How much" his friend asks. And bless him to this day, he replies "depends how hard I work" He was 9 or 10 at the time. How I kept a straight face I will never know. Inside I'm shouting YES ! The boy's learnt the only lesson he ever needs to know, input equals output.

...BOY, HAVE I WORKED HARD THIS WEEK!

My son has the advantage of being dyslexic, so his spatial awareness is astonishing, if I lose any thing in the house I can ask him, and after a moments soft focus while he examines the whole house in his head, he tells me where my phone or keys or wallet are.

He is however, not the most enthusiastic reader. However after finding out the rules of his trust fund were, that he had to save 30 % of his net P 60 income, until he was 35, he read "The Richest Man in Babylon" to understand the concept. This book should be compulsory reading for kids.

Quoted by many wealthy people, as the catalyst that got them started, this is one of the best financial strategy books I have ever read.

Within a week he had opened his own Issa saving account, and this year has saved £3500, as well as paying his Mother housekeeping, run his own car and saved and paid for his own holiday. He did this by studying for, and getting an additional job working Saturdays for his company, and doing odd jobs, like mowing lawns, and cleaning cars.

I am convinced this all came from introducing him as the kid who was smart with money when he earned his first pocket money, and saved half of it.

Now he is a smart kid so it shouldn't take him long to figure out that if he follows the plan, with smart management, and the power of compounding, when he gets to 35 he won't need a trust fund, because he will have built his own.

"Evidence based strength centered feedback"

You see on the back of my "Embarrass the kids " tee-
shirt it says :

"and spending their inheritance while I do"
and they think I'm joking.

My focus when I discovered that my most important
goal was to be a great dad, was to work myself out of a
job. To create the space and trust in which they could
grow to be their own independent person.

Speaking to the subconscious

I had a group of 14 year old school kids visit our
manufacturing facility in London.
At the end of the factory tour their teachers asked if I
would have a few moments to speak to them.
So I started by asking each of them what they wanted
to do when they finished school. Now if you have never
tried this, or have no experience of 14 year olds, or can't
remember what it was like to be 14, then you may not
find this story strange in the least. For those of you who
have or can. I promise this is a true story.

So I ask the first student what he wanted to do when
he leaves school, he says "Dunno" So I say "I know you

dunno, but if you did know, what would it be" "Chef" he says, just like that. We have a few moments on Jamie Oliver, and Ready Steady Cook and he's smiling. Next student, "so what are you going to do"

"I'm not sure really"

"I know you're not really sure but if you were really sure, what would it be" "Hair stylist" So we have this Vidal Sassoon moment, I tell her I've seen Paul Mitchell's private house in Hawaii, and her shoulders square and she looks down her nose at the people who sniggered, when she said, hair stylist.

There were 16 kids in that room, I got every one of them to tell me what they really wanted to do.
Two of the kids dug their heels in an gave me the
"I really don't have any idea"
So I get a little more devious and really speak to their subconscious mind, and ask.

"If you have to have an idea now, which one would you choose"

"Vet... I want to work with animals"

he almost shocked himself.
"What will you do if you can't be a vet"

"Well I like design, I always wanted to do something in design"

So I got him from, "I don't know", to having two ideas, with one question.

If we break down the second question I asked, there were two imbedded commands in it which spoke to the subconscious. They were "If you _HAVE TWO_ and _HAVE AN IDEA NOW_, which one would you choose"

It was easier for his subconscious, to do as I told it, and _HAVE TWO_ ideas, then chose which one to tell me about, than it was to try and make sense of the question. I must admit I asked him what the other idea was just to see if the first embedded command, "_HAVE TWO_" had worked.

When we finished the two teachers were shaking their heads in bemusement. As they left they told me the kids had had a careers advice session the day before, and none of them had come up with an idea of what they wanted to do when they left school.

I suspect the reason, was the careers advisor probably spoke to the kids conscious mind, and their minds probably weren't. I was also lucky in that I got a couple who picked careers in which I knew some cool people. So the other kids were more keen to have me say something cool about the things they wanted to do, it's positive peer pressure.

So if you want to know what people really want, speak to their subconscious mind, it knows everything and has all the answers.

How is that possible, that your subconscious mind knows so much? I read somewhere that the subconscious mind, and nervous system deal with over 2 million bits of information a second, that blew both my minds. Now although I haven't counted, let's accept it's a lot. So I tried one night to focus on as many sounds as I could hear in the house, at the same time.

Try this yourself it's a good mind stretch.

I had the dishwasher in the background, there was quiet music on, I could hear next doors kids playing in the garden, my pen scratching on the page, there was this strange background hiss, which almost felt like the sound of silence, if you know what I mean, and faintly, a clock ticking. I tried to listen to all that at the same time, and still hear each sound as an individual sound. It's really useful, in the office, my staff can't work out how I can be on the phone, in my office, and still hear what's going on in the main office.

I then added all the things I could feel, all the different pressure points on my body, I got up to about 6 distinct different points, then I started to notice what I could see, and now it's really getting difficult to concentrate.

Then Linda came in and asked me a question and I could only concentrate on one thing. The point is that for my conscious mind to become aware of each individual thing, my subconscious must have been aware of everything, and allowed through only the few things I focused on. If your <u>conscious</u> mind was aware of everything it would go mad. Just think for a moment about the huge amount of data that has to be processed, just to enable you to catch something. You have to compute a trajectory path, calculate a speed times trajectory, to establish a given point in space, that the object will be in, at a given time. You then have to calculate which muscles will be needed to move you into position, and which hand, you will use. You also, recognise the object in a fraction of a second, decide if it's heavy or fragile, then calculate how far to continue to follow the trajectory, once the object touches your hand, whilst calculating a rate of deceleration to save both your hand, and the object.

<u>WOW</u>!

Said you were amazing didn't I.

The thing is, you don't think about that process at all, it's all done subconsciously, with one instruction from the conscious, "Catch that" and I'll give you one guess what happens when the instruction is "don't drop it"

So in it's simplest form the subconscious is a filter, it sees hears and feel everything, it knows everything that you have ever done, smelt, tasted, heard, said, seen or felt, and all it wants to know is, what you want it to filter down to your conscious. If you don't give it clear instructions it will guess, and one of it's jobs is to make you right.

It hears "I can't believe how mean people are" "everybody's so rude these days" "I don't think my boss likes me" With those beliefs and instructions it wanders into your minds database of experience, looking for support to those statements.

And with all that information coming in, do you think it will have any trouble finding supporting references? Of Course not.

You buy a new car and suddenly everybody's driving the same car. i.e Now you're concious of THAT make.

So be careful what you focus on, "You may get it."

psst.... that was profound

How does this help you as a coach, well for yourself or your client, just being aware you have this fantastic tool that knows all the answers, means that all you have to do is work out the questions. The questions that focus on what you WANT.

And the wheel is all questions.

You may be one of those people, who read all through a work book like this, then go back and do the work, or you may have done all the work, as you went through. Which ever way you work, I hope you got and gave all you needed.

Two memories, do however, spring to mind, I was once asked by a coach I had trained "what was the best coaching tool I had come across." My subconscious mind saved me, and gave me the answer, and I said.

"A client" and I'm fairly sure I never learn as much as when I'm working with a real client.

Also I remember Richard Bandler said at a training I was attending, (when the group had been given instructions to go do a practical session), "you're all sitting there looking stunned, you think you need to understand this before you can do it,..... you need to go do it, then you'll understand it"

So keep doing it, and if so far you have only read the book, firstly, thank you. Secondly, a challenge, now go do all the work.

There was one main reason for keeping this book short other than keeping it simple. I wanted to have some one say to me one day "I've just finished your book and..."

So here it is, we're nearly done. I have touched on a number of subjects, and made some bold statements, and given you one or two of my thoughts, and shared some of my stories, stick with me to the end.

" A Client "

Never give up your dreams

Zig Ziglar tells a story about the Chinese bamboo tree which if you plant one and water and fertilize it in the first year does nothing. Water and fertilize it in the second year and nothing happens, third year, nothing, fourth year, water and fertilizer, nothing. Fifth year... Nothing ! but sometimes in the sixth year if you're lucky, the Chinese bamboo tree grows ninety feet in six weeks. Now the question is did it grow ninety feet in six years or six weeks, because if at any time in those six years you had forgotten to water and fertilize it, there would have been no growth at all.

For 15 years I've had a file with "Nics book" written on it, my first computer, and every computer since has had a "Nics book" file in it, for the first nine or ten years, the file was empty. Then slowly I started to jot the odd idea down, this carried on for the next three or four years.

Then people started to ask if I had written one, then they started to suggest I should write one.

Now it took me at least ten years of being a speaker, to get to the stage, where people said nice things about my presentations. So the concept of writing a book, the first book, and having it out there with my name on it, without the opportunity to practice, scared me witless.

So I just kept collecting ideas, jotting down notes, and promising myself I would do it. Do you know I have four books that authors have sent me, with notes in them, to tell me that their book was written as a result of the motivation gained by completing my goals/wheel workshop.

And I was still just thinking about it.

Finally, and I must thank Chris Day for the constant encouragement, I sat down to put together the working chapters one Friday night, as I was due to meet with Chris the following week to start talking the book, so he could record it, and the pen just kept going. I didn't look up one idea, or check one note, (Which might be why this feels like my talks) I just kept writing..... For 8 hours, eventually my hand was so cramped I couldn't hold the pen. This was about six

o'clock Saturday morning, I'd started ten o'clock Friday night. I tried to go to bed, but the ideas just seemed to be exploding in my head, so I got up and went back to it. Forty eight hours later, with about six hours sleep, the bones were done.

By the way my client who phoned on the way to her meeting called back to say the meeting went fantastic, and she had been totally calm and in control. I expected nothing less!

Sorry to interrupt, knew you would want to know.

Back to the story.... Now did it take fifteen years to write the book or forty eight hours?

I know I would like to say thank you for all the water and fertilizer along the way. To every one of you who said I should do this. I couldn't have done it without you.

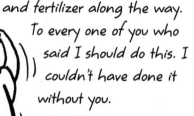

"Never let anyone steal your dream, especially yourself"

As I said at the beginning, this book was never meant to be the '7 point plan on how to live your life,' or the new '5 steps to wealth and happiness', not even the next 'how to win friends' manual.

Its sole objective was to pass on my version of the wheel, as a tool to help people gain focus, make decisions, find out what's important to them, and design their life, the way they want it to be.

I've indulged in sharing a little of my story along the way, in the hope it would underline the power of this process (if I can get from where I was to where I am now, anyone can)

I would like to leave you with two of my favourite quotes, borrowed from two of my favourite people.

Bilbo Baggins, who when it was time for him to go, said,

"I don't know half of you half as well as I should like; and I like less than half of you half as well as you deserve"

I do hope that's a compliment.

So send me your stories, fax me your wheels, share your
experiences with me, so I can get to know you as well as
you deserve.

My fervent wish...

Is that you should have a life, as lucky as mine.
To do what you love, for people who love what you do.

What could be better than that !

With all my love

<u>Nic</u>

Some people I would like to thank in no order;

To Linda, the love of my life. None of this would have been possible, without your quiet love, and continuous unquestioning belief and support. Thank you.

To my children Emily and Oliver, for being such a joy, and making me so proud, I love you always.

To Neil Tuson, author of The A to Z of Positive Thinking, A master of doing so himself. My mentor, coach and friend, and a continuous source of inspiration.

To my Mum, and number one fan, just for being my mum. You always made me feel good to be me.

To my Father. Dad, if I took the whole book I couldn't tell you what you've meant to me. A multi talented inspiration, and one of the kindest, most honest men I have ever met. A man with as much energy and passion for living and learning at 76 as he had at 26.
Thanks C.J.

To my Sister who has always loved what I've done, thanks Sis.

To Chris Day who has been my greatest encourager, and friend, a man who faces every challenge no matter how large with the most positive outlook of anyone I know, nothing has ever been too much trouble, and all the acknowledgement in the world would be half what he deserved. Thank you for your belief in me, I am honoured by it.

To every one of you who said I should, and all of you who thought I could, thank you.

To the coaches I have worked with and the trainers whose team I have been a part of, Vicki, Neil, and Sarah, it's been a joy.

To John, always there with the right tune and a supporting smile.

Some ideas on how else you... ...could use the wheel.

I have used it as a facilitation tool to run problem solving meetings.

Each of the 8 segments represent a cause of the problem, 0 to 10 measures the significance of the problem, the next circle of segments could contain possible solutions, next circle actions to be taken. The last part could be expected results.

A green light thinking tool following identification of a problem.

A sales training needs identification tool.

List all the sales skills necessary to do the job in each segment, measure current effectiveness of each of those skills. Mark each area 0 to 10 In the next circle list the action required to improve the skill. Next circle list the expected result, ie improved rapport, better closing, repeat sales, referrals. Next circle schedule training times.

You can then use the wheel to monitor the training progress, and record the results achieved.

The other way to use the wheel to to look at life issues in more detail is to do a wheel on each area of the first wheel. For example a health segment could have 8 areas on a new wheel.

Weight, exercise, diet, knowledge, motivation, planning, etc

A Family section could break down into, Wife son, daughter, dad, mum sister brother Parents-in-law cousins uncles, etc, each one of those could also be broken down into further sections. For example a Son wheel could consist of Dad, friend, coach, mentor, teacher, guide, role model. When you start to get into this at this sort of detail level your subconscious mind has to work much harder, but it gets better at it. When you coach and your client picks an area to work on just get them to draw another wheel for that section and ask what are all of the aspects of that area they could work on. Keep chunking down until they have a detailed plan of action in the key significant areas that will make the biggest fastest difference.

Oh yeah do this for yourself as well, ... GOOD LUCK